Rocks Into Gold

How software development teams can survive, then thrive, during the Credit Crunch

A Biztech Parable

by Clarke Ching

Copyright © 2009 by **Clarke Ching**

All rights reserved by the author. No part of this publication may be reproduced, stored in a retrieval system or transmitted in any form or by any means electronic, mechanical, photocopying, recording or otherwise, without the prior written permission of the author.

ISBN: 978-0-9561505-0-9

"I found it very thought provoking - it made me think about how my firm creates and presents an offering to a client."

Mark Woeppel, Author "Projects in Less Time:: A Synopsis of Critical Chain" and "Manufacturer's Guide to Implementing the Theory of Constraints"
pinnacle-strategies.com

"Clarke - You've got real skill at *saying* the simplest thing that could possibly work to get people's thinking shifted over to more fundamental ideas that can't help but inspire action. Thanks so much - I will recommend this little book!"

Nancy Van Schooenderwoert, Agile coach specializing in embedded systems
leanagilepartners.com

"Clarke is a good story-teller ... I particularly like the lessons he offers from theory of constraints and lean perspectives. Many people will miss it. That's ok. It's a story not a lecture. They won't miss that there is a way they can bring more value to their clients while increasing the cash flow for their firm. Nice job Clarke.

Hal Macomber, Project Reformer (and well-known blogger)
reformingprojectmanagement.com

Clarke Ching

1 Upset

Bob Billington was upset. Bob worked for KillerWattSoftware. His job title was "senior designer" although he thought of himself as a really good programmer. He was good at his job and he liked his job, but right now it looked like he might lose his job. At least, that's what Bob's boss, Sam, had said when she called Bob and the rest of the team into the conference room earlier that day.

Sam said, 'MegaCorp's management have given us formal notice that they are likely to cancel the Flitzerboing-Ultra project. Consumers are tightening their belts, global demand for Flitzerboings is down, down, down, and MegaCorp says that the Flitzerboing-Ultra project is no longer commercially viable.'

She explained that the loss of this important project meant that KillerWattSoftware suddenly didn't have enough money coming in, and it risked financial ruin. Nothing was certain, she said, but it looked like they may have to "let some of you go". She then handed everyone an envelope, said that the envelope was only a formality, and no final decision had been made yet. She said she was sorry to be the bearer of such bad news and uncertainty, then terminated the meeting.

Bob felt sorry for Sam - he knew that it wasn't nice to have to give such bad news - so he waited until everyone else left the room, then when he and Sam were alone he said, 'Tough day'.

'Yeah. Not much we can do about it, though, is there?' she answered.

She opened her jacket and pointed to an envelope sticking up out of the inside pocket. She shrugged and continued, 'We're all in the same boat.'

Bob was disappointed by the news, but his two boys were adults now and they had left home, he had paid off his mortgage, and even though his retirement savings were invested in the stock market, he knew he had enough money to see him through any rough times, if he was careful. He knew that Sam had two young kids at home. He knew that she and her husband had just moved into a fancy new house. He also knew without being told that someone upstairs in the HR department had already started preparing a spreadsheet, which would be used to objectively figure out who would be the most expensive to "let go". Bob had worked here for fifteen years, he got paid a lot and he was, he thought, irreplaceable – he knew the products, he knew the code, he knew where the skeletons were buried. Sam had worked here for three years, she didn't get paid nearly as much as Bob, and, not to put too fine a point on it, project managers were a dime a dozen. The math wasn't hard. Bob felt sorry for Sam.

Bob didn't know what to say, so he just said, 'Yeah,' and they walked out of the room together.

2 Consequences

Sam went upstairs and Bob went back to his desk, where he opened the envelope. It contained a letter from Eugene "Killer" Watt, it was on formal letterhead paper, and it told Bob nothing he hadn't already figured out; expect that a formal announcement would be made in two weeks time.

Bob shrugged, but rather than turning to the job websites like he knew many of his younger colleagues were now doing, he fired up Google news. He sat there for half an hour, watching the headlines change as the website automatically refreshed every few minutes. He hoped a new headline would pop up saying that this whole recession thing was over. Nothing changed. Bob didn't expect it to. He had been around long enough to recognise the pattern. There were always a number of good years, prosperous years, where the stock market slowly rose up, up and away, until suddenly, out of the blue, it crashed back down. Everyone expressed surprise, shock, and horror; the media talked about little else; house prices dropped, unemployment went up; then slowly, things got better; the stock market slowly rose up, up and away; this went on for a few more years, the world got prosperous again, and then suddenly, out of the blue ...

Bob closed his browser window and fired up his email client. He had loads of work to do. Sam had said that, officially, the Flitzerboing-Ultra project was still active until they heard otherwise. Bob opened up an email from Peter Prince. Peter was a designer at MegaCorp. He did much the same job as Bob did and they had worked together, off and on, for the last four years. More recently, Peter and Bob had gone back and forth a lot during the last two months, working out the specifications of the Flitzerboing-Ultra software.

Peter had sent the email late the previous

evening. Peter had answered some, but not all of Bob's questions; he had promised to send the remaining answers later in the week. That was fine with Bob, because the important questions had been answered and he could get on with his own work.

Bob reread the email and realised that when he wrote it, Peter had no idea that the project was going to be cancelled. Had Peter and his workmates just been given a bunch of envelopes too? Bob knew that Peter would be very upset by the news, because he was looking forward to buying the Flitzerboing-Ultra for his granny as a gift for her on her 99th birthday. Perhaps, Bob thought, the economy might pick up sooner rather than later, and she might get it for her 100th birthday.

3 Why are MegaCorp Cancelling the Project?

Sam walked by. Bob called her over.

'Sam,' he asked. 'Explain to me again why MegaCorp can't afford to pay us to build the FBU.'

Being of a technical disposition, Bob and his team referred to the Flitzerboing-Ultra by the initials FBU. Sam did too, but only when she was talking with her team. She always used the full name when she was talking with MegaCorp people – they took things like that very seriously. She had heard a rumour that MegaCorp had paid an upmarket marketing agency over $150,000 to come up with the name Flitzerboing-Ultra. Considering that the

Flitzerboing series had been around for a dozen years, one hundred and fifty grand seemed a lot just for adding the word Ultra.

Sam replied, 'It's all about money: revenue and cost. Businesses and consumers are worried about money, so they're tightening their belts; spending less. FBU isn't the sort of product people buy when they're tightening their belts. MegaCorp believe that sales - revenue - across the entire Flitzerboing product range will drop by between 25 and 50%. That's a big hit.'

Bob said nothing. He thought about what Sam said. What applied to MegaCorp also applied to KillerWattSoftware. FBU represented, what, a quarter of KillerWattSoftware's revenue for the forthcoming year. If many more projects were cancelled, the company could fold.

'Yikes,' said Bob.

'Yikes indeed,' agreed Sam.

Bob asked, 'Well, couldn't we charge them a little less for our work? KillerWattSoftware may not make as much money from the deal, but at least we'd save the project, earn some money, and perhaps we'd save a few jobs.'

'Our account manager tried to negotiate with MegaCorp. Apparently, they offered them a 20% reduction, but the MegaCorp guys just laughed at them. They said that that represented only a tiny drop in their ocean of troubles,' Sam answered,

Bob raised an eyebrow. Twenty percent sounded like a good discount to him. But what did he know about such things? He reminded himself that he was a programmer not a businessman.

Hmmmm.

'Can't MegaCorp just drop *their* prices? They might earn more money if the price were lower and more people bought it.'

Sam said, 'I guess they could ... but pricing is a tricky thing. They might make more by lowering the price; they might make less. Seriously! It's not so straightforward. Besides, if they drop their prices, then so will their competitors. They could end up starting a price war, which no one except the consumer wants.'

Bob nodded. The folk at MegaCorp were good businesspeople. He was sure they had thought about these sorts of options. At the end of the day, it wasn't up to a bunch of computer programmers to suggest to well-seasoned business people how to run their businesses.

Bob summarised, 'So, MegaCorp reckon they can't make enough money from the FBU project, and therefore we will probably lose our jobs.'

Sam said, 'Yeah' and wandered off. She had a Gantt chart to polish.

4 Yes but ...

Bob turned back to his computer, reread Peter Prince's email then fired up his word processor. It seemed utterly pointless now, but he needed to update some of the FBU project documentation based on Peter's email.

A few moments later, his inter-office messaging software started flashing at him indicating he had a new message. He clicked on the flashing icon and the message popped up. It was from Billy. It simply said, 'Bollocks!"

Billy sat in the cubical opposite Bob, but he preferred communication via keyboard rather than via lip.

Bob stood up just enough that he could see

Billy on the other side of the cubicle divider. Bob asked, 'What's wrong Billy?'

Billy didn't look up, instead he typed faster. Bob wasn't offended. Billy wasn't being rude, he was just being Billy. Billy was a modern man: he had lots of friends all around the world, and thanks to the Internet, he could interact with them without ever having to talk to them. In fact, Billy held celebrity status amongst some of the more technically inclined Internet tribes, where he was known as BinaryBilly.

Bob sat down again and waited a couple of seconds until his inter-office messaging software popped up again.

Billy had written, 'What Sam said is bollocks. MegaCorp aren't cancelling FBU because people won't buy it. That just doesn't compute.' Billy had obviously been listening in to Bob and Sam's discussion.

Bob replied, 'Why'd u say that?'

'The people on the news say this recession might last a year, perhaps two at most, and then things will start to pick up. You and I know that FBU won't be on sale for at least eighteen months. By the time it does ship, things are likely to be picking up.'

Hmmm, thought Bob. *That made sense.*

Another message popped up. 'IMNSHO MegaCorp are crazy to cancel FBU now. They'd be far better off continuing with the project and then launching it, as planned, when the bad times are turning good again.'

Hmmm, thought Bob. *Billy had a point.*

He wrote back, 'So, why are MegaCorp really cancelling the project?'

He heard Billy typing, then moments later saw his answer. 'It must be because they're stupid.'

Bob knew that wasn't true. He had been dealing with them for years and they weren't stupid.

He picked up his phone.

5 Cash Shortage

'Peter Prince speaking.'

Bob said 'hi', made an appropriate amount of small talk, then got to the point.

'Why are MegaCorp really cancelling FBU?'

Peter, being a technical kinda guy, also referred to the Flitzerboing-Ultra as FBU. He did this deliberately. Partly to annoy the marketing guys, but mostly because he didn't see the point of wasting syllables or keystrokes.

Peter gave a very direct, but at the same time circuitous answer to Bob's very direct question. 'We're not getting enough money in from our existing products. We don't have enough cash in our bank accounts, and the bosses are afraid we won't be able to pay our bills. The bosses have given all contractors their obligatory notice, but no permanent staff have been laid off – so far. The financial guys are selling the buildings we work in, and then renting them back from the people they sold them to. Our Christmas party has been cancelled this year, we're not getting paid bonuses, and they're cancelling a whole lot of projects, including FBU.'

Bob understood. 'So, it doesn't matter how much money FBU will bring in when it launches. If it takes money out of MegaCorp's bank accounts, then it's dangerous and has to be killed?'

'That's it. There's even a rumour that the marketing guys will have to downgrade from first to business class whenever they fly. That's unheard of.'

'Thanks Peter,' said Bob.

He wasn't sure if Peter should have told him all that, but it helped. He hung up then composed a quick email to Billy explaining the situation.

There wasn't anything Bob could do about the state of the economy, so he went back to his work, updating design documents for a dead-duck project that was still, officially, quacking.

6 Cash Flow in More Detail

Later that day, after he had eaten his lunch, Bob spotted Sam coming back into the office. She walked over to her desk, dropped off her handbag and then came straight over to Bob's desk. She crouched down beside him and said, 'You know, I think I gave you the wrong answer this morning. MegaCorp want to cancel FBU because they don't have enough cash to pay for it.'

Bob nodded. One of the things he liked about Sam is that she freely admitted when she had made a mistake. He didn't say he had figured it out himself.

Sam continued, 'Let me explain. Imagine that the MegaCorp financial guys set up a special bank account for the FBU project. Now,

I don't know their numbers, and some of the numbers are unknowable, but I can take a rough guess at them. If they don't cancel the project, then they'll have to keep paying us roughly half a million dollars each month for the next year before they launch the product and make some money.'

Bob said, 'Ah ha.'

In his vast experience, most twelve-month long projects took eighteen months, but he said nothing. Much of the last six months had been taken up by changing the software so that it did what the customer wanted, not what they asked for. KillerWattSoftware made much of its money from those change requests.

Sam said, 'I imagine MegaCorp's other internal costs would be about the same. So, let's say that it costs a cool million a month to fund the project. That means they have to spend twelve million on this project before it goes live and they can sell the FBU product.'

Bob said, 'So that's $12,000,000 out of their special FBU bank account before they make any money. That's a big overdraft, Sam!'

'Precisely!' Sam answered. 'And right now, at a time when everyone is tightening their belts, no one has that kind of cash available to spare.'

Bob nodded. He grabbed a blank sheet of paper and a pen then drew a quick graph. He wrote "Bank Balance" on the Y axis and "Months" on the X axis, then drew a line showing the balance decreasing month-on-month for the next twelve months. He turned to show it to Sam.

She smiled and said, 'You've got it. Now, let me show you what happens in month thirteen, when they start selling the FBU product.'

She pulled her own pen from her jacket pocket, then drew a line going up, up and away, at a surprisingly steep slope. It re-crossed the X axis at month eighteen.

'In theory, if the economy hadn't crashed and this project had continued on, then the FBU product was predicted to sell very well indeed. I don't know the real numbers, but our business guys estimated that it would bring in around two million dollars profit each month once it went live. The project would "break even" six months after it went live - that's the point where the bank account crossed over from a negative to a positive balance. Of course, that number was just a forecast - an educated guess, it could be more, it could be less - but you get the idea.'

'Wow,' said Bob, neatly expressing his amazement. He had pretty much ignored the money side of a project when it had been mentioned previously; his job was to make software, not money, after all.

Out of the corner of his eye, he saw his inter-office messaging software flash. He moved the mouse of the icon and saw that the latest message was from Billy. It said, 'Double WOW!'

'You think that's wowable? Those numbers are conservative. MegaCorp is a big company and because of its scale, it can make huge revenue from relatively small investments.'

Bob hmmmmed again. 'So, in the long run, MegaCorp is losing a lot of money by not doing FBU?'

Sam said, 'Yeah,' then wandered off. She had some I's to dot and several T's to cross before home time.

Bob tore the page off his pad then pinned it up on his cubicle wall. He hmmmmed once more; his retirement fund had shares in MegaCorp.

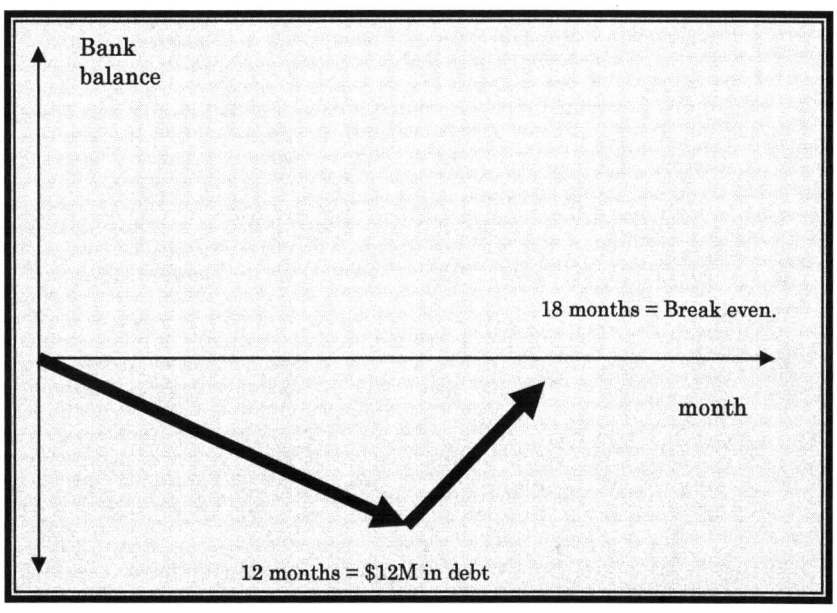

7 Brief Bit Where Bob does Nothing

He went back to work on his pointless FBU documentation. Updating it. FBU was a great product; there was no doubting that. Shame it would never exist.

As soon as he had finished, he checked his email. His eyes were drawn to an email from his favourite online bookseller. He had ordered three books but one of them was delayed. They were going to ship the two books that were available right away, which Bob was thankful for, because two books was surely more useful than none. Then they were going to ship the other book to him in a couple days time, when it became available. They were going to swallow the extra shipping charge too - a small gesture which pleased Bob.

8 How Could We Make this Situation Worse?

When Bob got to his desk the following day, his two books were there waiting for him. He tore open the packaging with childlike glee. One of the books was a technical book about a programming language Bob was learning in his spare time; the other was a science fiction novel. They were nothing to do with his job, but he had them posted to the office so he could enjoy moments like these without his wife asking him where he was going to put the books. His house was already full of books. His garden shed was full of books. His wife called it his "library". Bob loved books. He sniffed the newness of his new books, then put them in his carry bag. *Tonight, my darlings, you are mine.*

Bob logged into his computer then skimmed his emails. Nothing urgent so he logged on to the booksellers' website and cancelled the book that hadn't shipped yet. It was a book about beekeeping, something Bob was interested in only on a purely theoretical level. He felt sad as he cancelled the book order, but he figured it was better to have that money in the bank given the current uncertainty with his job and his income. The bookseller would miss his money less than he would - unless, of course, other people whose jobs were at risk were also cancelling their book orders. Bob hoped the bookseller would be okay.

Bob had made a decision earlier that morning while on his way to work. He had decided to learn more about the financial side of the FBU project. He called Gwendolyn, who managed KillerWattSoftware's relationship with MegaCorp, and asked her if she could spare him ten minutes. Bob didn't understand the difference between a "relationship manager" and a "salesperson" nor did he care. Gwendolyn told him, in her delightful and friendly way, that she always welcomed visits from the troops, and that he should make his way upstairs.

Bob carefully avoided making small talk with Gwendolyn. He had heard she did a lot of networking in her evenings, but he was a software, not a hardware guy, so he avoided the topic. Unless she was a hobby apiarist[1] then it seemed unlikely they would have anything in common to chat about. He came straight out with his question.

'What would have happened if the economy hadn't crumbled, the FBU project wasn't cancelled, and it took twenty-four months to deliver the project rather than twelve months?

Gwendolyn took a few moments to parse his question, then looked at him suspiciously. It seemed odd to her that one of the technical staff would be asking such a question. Bob didn't realise or even care if the question sounded odd. He was trying to solve a problem and over the years, he had found that oftentimes the key to improving a difficult situation was to figure out

---

[1] A beekeeper.

what would make it worse and then do the opposite.

Gwendolyn put aside her suspicions and answered, 'Well, Bob, obviously I don't know the real numbers and nor do MegaCorp - they can't predict the future - but before the current crisis, we estimated that they would make around two million dollars profit each month, once it went live. So, to answer your question, if the economy hadn't collapsed but the project had run twelve months late, then MegaCorp would have lost twenty-four million dollars profit.'

'Maybe more, maybe less?' Bob asked.

'Uh huh. That's right.'

'How about us? What would KillerWattSoftware lose?'

'Well, we'd have had to pay very, very, very high penalty charges. MegaCorp made it very clear in the negotiations that the profitability of the FBU product depended on getting it to market as soon as possible. Now, this might sound crazy - if you didn't know how much money they stood to make – but MegaCorp were willing to pay us *more money* if we delivered

FBU in six months than we are receiving by delivering it in twelve months.'

Bob was about to say, 'But that's crazy! Why would they pay more when it took us less time, less effort?' But he didn't because he knew the answer. MegaCorp were willing to pay KillerWattSoftware more because they would end up with loads more money, something like $12M extra in their bank account. It was only a little different to paying a furniture company a little extra to deliver on a Saturday because it was convenient.

Gwendolyn added, 'But we're not cowboys. We knew we couldn't make that commitment and keep to it. So we didn't.'

Bob nodded. He had been part of the team that had put together the 12-month estimate. They had taken the product specifications to pieces and estimated that they could deliver the project in nine to ten months. Gwendolyn and her colleagues had bumped that estimate up to twelve months. Bob realised that they had built in a little safety to protect themselves from the killer penalty clauses. That made sense.

Bob had one last question. 'I know things aren't so good now, and they might not be for a while, but would MegaCorp still make money from FBU if by some miracle it did go live in twelve – or even six – months time? I mean, apart from the cash situation, the FBU product is still commercially viable, right?'

Gwendolyn smiled, 'Of course. Even if they only sold half of what they previously expected, they'd still make loads of money from the product.'

Bob thanked Gwendolyn for her time. She, in her bubbly, salesperson way, said, 'Sure, no problem, any time.' Bob went back downstairs to his desk, wondering as he walked, why he had never been aware of FBU's financial implications before. Sometimes, it felt like KillerWattSoftware's left hand didn't know what its right hand was doing.

9 Bob's Lightbulb Moment

Bob sat at his desk and thought.

He thought briefly about the two books he had ordered, then smiled.

Then he thought about the third book and frowned.

Then he had a brainwave.

And then he thought that his brainwave was

just crazy. It was too obvious to be plausible; otherwise everyone would already be doing it. But they weren't. Were they?

He fired up his inter-office messaging system and sent a message to Billy, 'You got a minute?'

Ninety minutes later, Billy and Bob concluded that Bob's brainwave was, technically speaking, sound. They also concluded that there were only two reasons why they had never done this before.

The first reason was that no one had ever asked them to do it before, so they had never had bothered to think about it.

The second reason was that their jobs had never been on the line like this before.

10   Include Others to Make the Solution Better

Bob picked up his phone and called Peter Prince.

'How are things at MegaCorp?'

'Glum,' said Peter. 'All of my get up and go has got up and gone. And you know what? I think it took my will to live along with it.'

'Same here. Imminent financial disaster does that to you,' said Bob. 'However, I've got an idea that might just save our jobs. I need to run it by you, off the record, first.'

They agreed to meet later that evening.

Bob spent the next two hours editing a spreadsheet they had used to prepare the project estimates earlier that year. Once he had finished that, he went to Sam's desk and asked her to join him for a coffee at the Starbucks across the street. As they walked to the coffee shop, Bob explained his cunning plan. Thirty minutes later, Sam, with the aid of a couple of shots of caffeine, had not only bought into the brainwave, but had helped Bob put a "commercial" shine on it. By the time they made it back to the office "Bob's brainwave" had become "Sam and Bob's solution". Bob didn't mind, the more people who felt like they owned this idea, the more likely it was to succeed.

Bob then went to talk to Charlie, their usability expert, and asked him a few pertinent questions. Charlie's answers surprised him at first, but then when he thought about them a little, they made perfect sense.

Just before he left the office, Bob went back online and reordered his beekeeping book.

Fortunately, they had one in stock. Bob smiled.

11 Even Talk to the Customer!

Bob bought Peter and himself a beer, then the two of them took their drinks over to a table in the far corner of the bar.

Bob fired up his laptop and showed him the spreadsheet. He said that the spreadsheet was a list of all FBU's features and requirements.

Peter said he understood, but he couldn't see what the spreadsheet had to do with saving his job.

Bob said he would do his best to explain. But first, he asked a question. 'Am I right in saying that even in today's economic climate, if it weren't for the shortage of spending money, FBU would still be a commercially viable product?'

'Of course.'

'Good. In that case, I want to show you how, with just a little bit of planning, you and I can figure out how to do this project with far, far, far, less cash. I think that we can not only save our jobs, but I'm certain that with just a little extra work this week, we can make your bosses more money than they ever expected to.'

Peter looked sceptical but he had known Bob long enough to know he was trustworthy, intelligent, and not the sort of man to waste a fellow designer's time. He asked Bob to tell him more.

Bob said, 'I want to add one new requirement to your project that reads something like this: "KillerWattSoftware shall deliver the most important features to MegaCorp in a saleable state three months after the start of the project. And then they shall deliver the remaining features in three more, similarly-sized, prioritised mini-projects – one every three months."'

'Whoa there, Killer,' said Peter. 'That's quite a mouthful, dude. I don't know what you mean.'

'Sorry, Mega,' said Bob. 'Let me translate from formal requirements language into normal English. What I mean is this: instead of delivering one big project which takes a full year, I want to deliver four smaller projects, each of which takes around three months. The first mini-project delivers FBU 1.0, which you guys sell and earn money - cash - from. It will be built to the same standard we'd always produce – MegaCorp worthy as you say, but it will only have the most valuable features. The second mini-project delivers FBU 1.1. It has more features, attracts even more customers, and brings in even more cash. And then we do the third and the forth project.'

Peter screwed up his nose. 'That doesn't make sense, dude! Who'd buy a quarter of a product?'

Bob said, 'According to Charlie, our usability expert, you could turn off most of the features on most of the software we've shipped at KillerWattSoftware, and no one would notice or care because no one ever uses them. He's done studies. It's called the 80 / 20 principle: 80% of the value in the software comes from 20% of the product.' Bob pointed at the spreadsheet and said, 'We think the same principle applies to FBU too.'

Peter took another slurp from his beer. He said, 'Nuts!'

Bob frowned then said, 'Why's it nuts?'

'It's not nuts. I need nuts. This beer is making me crave salt.'

He got up and went to the bar. Bob figured that Peter didn't really want nuts; he just wanted time to absorb this crazy new idea. A minute later, Peter returned with a bowl of nuts. He sat down and said, 'Okay. I buy your argument - it makes sense technically. I mean to say, the first iPod didn't have half as many features as its competition, but it succeeded because it did what it did, very well. They added features over time, and more and more people bought it. And Google went live with Gmail when it was still a beta. They gave their customers a good product, loads of people started using it, they kept adding features and improving the service, and all that time, they were earning advertising revenue. I'm not qualified or authorised to judge your suggestion from a commercial viewpoint, but if your relationship manager proposes it to our business folk, then I'll support you from the technical point of view.'

'Great!' said Bob. He wished he had ordered two beekeeping books now.

Bob continued, 'Look, how about if we run some numbers on my laptop? I don't know, and I don't wanna know what your internal costs are, nor what your revenue predictions are, so we can just make some numbers up that feel good enough.'

Bob opened up the spreadsheet, and within ten minutes they had prepared a simple model of the FBU project's "bank account". Bob suggested they assume that the costs were a static one million dollars each month; that FBU 1.0 earned only three quarters of a million a month, FBU 1.1 earned a million a month, FBU 1.2 earned 1.2 million each month, and the final version earned 1.5 million each month. They had no idea if the numbers were valid, but the approach needed a whole lot less of MegaCorp's cash than the original plan, and it painted a far prettier picture than cancelling FBU. The previous plan, with just one release at the end of twelve months, meant that MegaCorp built up a $12,000,000 "debt". With the new plan, the most the project ever owed MegaCorp was $3,750,000. That was still a lot of money as far as Bob was concerned, but it was a lot less than $12,000,000. Who knew how real these numbers were? Only time would tell.

Peter, who was now driving the laptop, selected a few columns on the spreadsheet, clicked a button, and a graph appeared.

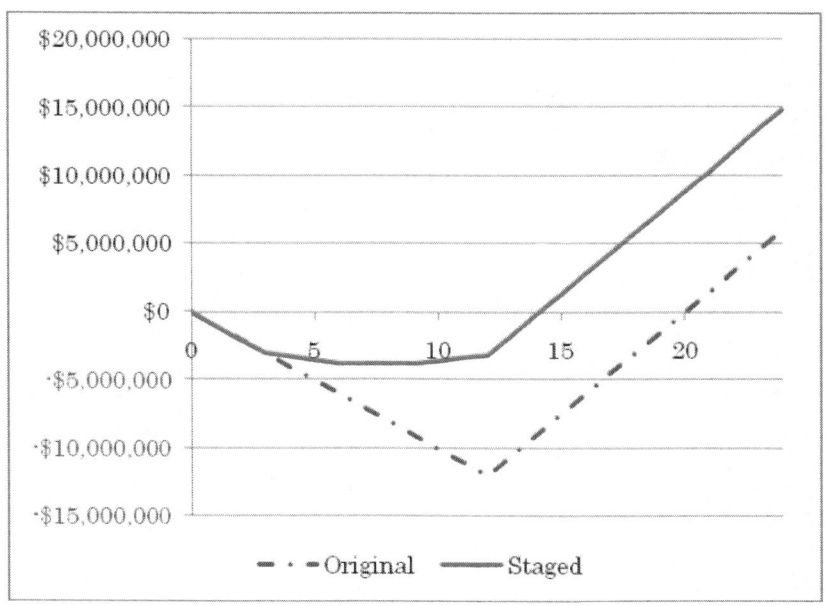

'Wow!' said Peter. 'You know how they say a picture is worth a 1,000 words?'

Bob agreed, 'I do.'

'Well, that picture right there might just be worth a few million dollars,' said Peter. 'And it might just save both our jobs.'

Bob nodded. 'Your granny will be pleased.'

Peter said, 'Yeah, she will. But look there. The FBU project pays for itself by the fifteenth month. If we'd done it the old way, with just one release, then MegaCorp wouldn't have gotten all of it's money back until the twentieth month.'

Bob pointed at the screen and said, 'You see that gap between the two lines. It seems to be constant. Can you figure out how much it is, Pete?'

Peter did a quick calculation with the spreadsheet then said, 'Eight million, eight hundred and fifty thousand dollars.'

'Does that mean that by making one tiny little change, like we've done here, that the FBU project would, for ever and ever, be

$8,850,000 better off?'

Peter said, 'You know what, Bob? I think it does.'

'And even though it's not the real number, it is real money, isn't it?'

'It is.'

'Wow!' said Bob. 'Wow. Would you like another beer?'

'I would,' said Peter, 'but let me get them.'

While Peter was at the bar, Bob thought how amazing it was that he, a simple programmer who didn't know or care all that much about money, could figure out something so simple and yet so important. Bob wasn't the sort of man who would count his chickens before they had hatched, but he allowed himself a tiny little congratulatory smile. Numbers talked and MegaCorp had good reason to listen.

When Peter returned, he put the two beers down on the table, hmmmmed, then said, 'One question for you: how do we figure out what goes into each mini-project?'

Bob asked Peter if he knew how to do a

"Quick Sort" and Peter looked at him as if he were mildly insulted, but then said of course he did. Bob knew he did, but he enjoyed teasing Peter. He told Peter that it would be far easier than doing a quick sort. The two of them spent the next forty minutes, with help from two more beers (one each - it was a work night) sorting the spreadsheet.

They used a simple divide and conquer approach. They made a quick first pass through the spreadsheet, classifying each requirement and feature as either a high or a low priority feature. They then sorted the spreadsheet so that the high priority features were at the top of the spreadsheet, and the lower priority features were at the bottom of the spreadsheet.

On their second pass through the spreadsheet, they prioritised all of the "high" priority features into "very high" and "high" and then, just for the fun of it, they reprioritised some of the "very highs" to "very, very highs". They decided to leave the low priority features for another day because, well, they didn't care - they had proven their point.

They were happy: they weren't trying to get the list perfect, just convince themselves that the concept was sensible. FBU's Product Manager would need to go through this process and decide on the final prioritisation.

Bob folded his laptop shut and put it in his bag. He asked Peter if he were still okay with the idea.

Peter said, 'Yes...and... ' then he scratched the back of his head and said, 'And you know what? I know we didn't sort the low priority features, but there's little point. By the time we get to thinking about mini-project number three, we'll have had some great feedback from customers who've been using FBU 1.0 in real life. No doubt we'll replace some of the features in the spreadsheet with more useful features. That'll save us paying you guys a fortune for change requests too!'

Bob smiled. Another benefit! Not only had he figured out a simple way to rescue FBU and his job ... but ... oh drat ... Bob gulped ... he had figured out a way to eliminate one of KillerWattSoftware's major revenue sources.

That wasn't going to go down to well back at the office.

He put on a brave face and said, 'Yeah.' They finished up their drinks and went off home.

12 Will They Buy It?

Bob arrived at work the following morning, slightly hung over, but thrilled with himself. He spied the beekeeping book sitting wrapped up in its cardboard wrapping, but he ignored it. Today, he had bigger fish to fry. He went straight to the conference room where Sam was waiting for him. Bob reported that his meeting had gone well with Peter. Sam suggested they go straight to Gwendolyn and make their proposal. Bob hesitated for a moment, wondering if he should mention the potential problem with the lost change control revenue. Bob wasn't good at keeping secrets so he spilled the beans. Sam understood the problem immediately. She said that the best they could do was to be completely open with Gwendolyn ... but to hold off on mentioning it until Gwendolyn understood the big picture.

They popped by Gwendolyn's desk. She wasn't there. They left a note and went back to their desks. Bob and Sam used the time to play around with his spreadsheet.

Two frustrating hours later, Bob spied Gwendolyn coming through the stairwell door.

Two minutes later, the three of them were in the conference room scratching out numbers on the whiteboard.

Thirteen minutes later, Gwendolyn said, 'I can sell this. You two have almost certainly just saved a load of jobs - both here and at MegaCorp.'

She threw down her marker pen, shouted out, 'Yippee-ki-yay,' then said, 'I've got to make some phone calls.'

She picked up her handbag and made to leave, but Bob stopped her and told her about Peter's plans to use the last mini project to handle change requests.

Gwendolyn frowned, bit down on her lip then smiled and said, 'A change pool? Ingenious! So, what you're saying is that not only do MegaCorp earn more money than they ever expected to, but they also get to change FBU and make it a better product and at the same time, remove the biggest source of friction between us?'

Bob nodded. He was confused. Didn't she understand the implications of what he had said? He said, 'But that means we will finish the project much earlier, and we can't charge MegaCorp for the change requests.'

'You are right, Bob. With the way we currently sell our services, that's a benefit for them and a risk for us. Equally, MegaCorp could, if they wanted to, stop the whole project after the first release. But don't worry about such things, my friend. MegaCorp have so, so, so much to gain by working this way that they're not going to haggle price with us. What you two have here is a truly compelling offer. I'm not going to sell them man-days at a competitive daily rate. Oh no, no, no, no, no. I'm going to sell them the opportunity to make bucket loads more money.'

She grabbed her handbag and said, 'Good work, Sam. Good work, Bob. I'll let you know what happens.'

Gwendolyn dashed out of the conference room. Bob and Sam looked at each other, shrugged, then went back to their work.

13 Long-term benefits

One week later, Bob was sitting at his desk helping one of the younger developers with some tricky code when Eugene "Killer" Watt, the founder and chairman of KillerWattSoftware, stopped by his desk. Bob had worked with Eugene since the early days, but a lot had changed since then and they didn't see so much of each other any more.

Eugene asked the young programmer to excuse them, then he asked Bob to take a walk with him. He didn't look happy. As soon as they were outside the building and out of earshot of Bob's colleagues, Eugene said, 'You know, Bob, MegaCorp didn't greet Gwendolyn's and my offer with quite the open arms we were expecting. Truth be known, they were downright hostile about it. Their marketing team said that they simply didn't have enough staff to handle three extra FBU releases over the next year. Their customer support director said that their phones went crazy whenever they released a new product and, like the marketing folk, he wasn't set up to handle the extra call volumes. And it turns out that your friend Peter Prince wasn't quite as keen on the idea once he'd sobered up. He was concerned about the extra coding work required to ensure that customers upgraded smoothly between releases.'

Bob said, 'But ... but ...' then he stopped. He looked down at the pavement in front of him and kept walking. He didn't know what to say to Eugene. Sure, MegaCorp and KillerWattSoftware's developers would have to do some extra coding work to handle the multiple upgrades, but it wasn't all that much relative to the size of the entire project, and Bob figured that the time saved from dropping the low priority features would more than compensate. He also knew that Sam and Peter's manager would need to do a little extra upfront planning and coordinating, but Sam had told him that she wasn't stressed about it. So Bob wasn't worried about the technical implications.

Bob's problem was that he had no solution to the marketing and customer service implications. In fact, he'd never even thought about them.

Eugene stopped walking, turned to Bob, smiled broadly, and said with a twinkle in his eyes, 'But ... when their Finance Director saw Gwendolyn's cash flow projections, he turned to me and said that although his colleagues had all expressed very valid objections, MegaCorp would figure out how to overcome them. He said that too many jobs and too much money was at stake to let a few little "details" get in the way.'

Bob's jaw dropped open as he processed Eugene's words. He tried to speak but words failed him yet again. For a brief moment, he resembled a goldfish trying to say his own name: Bob, Bob, Bob. MegaCorp had accepted Gwendolyn's new offer and now no one in KillerWattSoftware would lose their jobs! Bob's face broke into a smile.

Eugene added, 'There's just one thing. By the end of the meeting, MegaCorp decided to do three mini-projects, each taking about four months, rather than four mini-projects each taking about three months. Is that a problem?'

Bob said, 'Hmmm.' Three mini-projects? Four mini-projects? It made no difference to him. The folks at MegaCorp knew what they were doing. He told Eugene that was fine.

Eugene reached out and put his hand on Bob's arm. He said, 'Thank you, Bob.'

Bob shrugged and replied, 'My pleasure, Eugene.' He really didn't know what else to say. Strictly speaking, he knew that he had done more than his job required - he was a just programmer after all, albeit a very good one - but he liked to think that he had done *precisely* what any good, red-blooded developer would do under the circumstances.

Eugene turned, and he and Bob started walking back to the office. Eugene said he would like to repay Bob and asked him if there was anything he wanted or needed. Bob asked if, perhaps, if it wasn't asking too much, could

Eugene possibly arrange to get him a bigger monitor for his desk? Eugene said he would see what he could do, but he couldn't make any promises.

Bob figured that meant yes. He said, 'Okay,' and they slowly made their way back to the office, talking about the old days as they went.

Eugene stopped outside the office building and he asked Bob to explain just how he came up with this simple but devastatingly effective solution. Bob shrugged then said that he had just thought about things a lot, and tried to figure out how to solve his problem by solving other people's problems. The hardest part, he said, was figuring out what the other people's problems were. There wasn't much more to it than that, he told Eugene.

Eugene nodded then thanked Bob yet again. He graciously held the door open for Bob and let him into the building first. Bob gulped when he entered the room, and saw his colleagues all standing in a semi-circle facing him. Bob figured Sam must have told them the good news. They burst into applause. Bob smiled nervously then Sam said a few words. Thankfully, she didn't ask him to say anything, and a few moments later they all went back to their desks.

Eugene quietly thanked Bob once more then walked over to Sam and spoke to her for a moment before they both disappeared into the conference room.

Bob went back to his desk, picked up his phone, then called Peter Prince. He asked Peter if he had received the news.

Peter said, 'Killer! Dude! Have I heard the news? Everyone here has heard the news. You and me, we've saved the project and our jobs! We're heroes!'

Bob just answered, 'Okay.' He didn't want to be a hero.

'And guess what? Our managers here reckon that at least one-third of our projects can use your idea. Our Finance Director has demanded that every single project manager prioritises their project's features just like we did. And you know what? Even if we can't deliver a project in a piecemeal fashion, then we can probably chop *some* low-value features, deliver the project sooner, and get the MegaCorp cash registers ringing sooner. Man, we are going to be famous.'

'Cool ... ' said Bob half-heartedly. He wasn't all that interested in the money side of things now that his job was safe. He glanced at his watch. He really should get back to the young programmer he'd been helping before Eugene came downstairs.

Peter continued, 'And what's more, Dude – don't tell anyone this, but the big bosses are in a big meeting right now figuring out how to keep the idea secret from our competitors!'

Bob asked, 'Huh?'

'Yeah,' said Peter. 'We've found a way to tighten our belts AND keep moving forward at the same time. We want our competitors to just keep tightening their belts.'

Bob said, 'Cool', but he didn't mean it. He told Peter Prince that he had to go then he hung up.

Bob was upset.

Why would anyone want to keep such a

simple and sensible idea secret when it could cause so much good?

Bob sat at his desk thinking. He thought, and thought, and thought.

He didn't want to keep his idea secret. It didn't feel right.

What would people think of a doctor who discovered a powerful and cheap cure for a deadly disease, but then kept it secret? What about a cook who discovered a fantastically simple but delicious cookie recipe? Wouldn't she want to share it with the world? And wouldn't a good programmer always share a nifty new algorithm and not keep it from the world?

He thought and thought and thought some more.

Then he had another idea. He fired up his word processor. He typed and typed and typed and typed and typed and typed and typed and typed and typed and typed and typed and typed and typed and typed and typed.

Once he was happy with what he had written, he pinged Billy using the inter-office messaging software, 'BinaryBilly ... You there?'

'Where else would I be?'

'I've got something I want to share with the world. Can you help?'

'Surely, my friend.'

Bob smiled. He wasn't upset anymore.

About Clarke Ching

Clarke Ching is an independent consultant based in Scotland. He specialises in the application of Goldratt's Theory of Constraints to software development. He is chairperson of the AgileScotland special interest group, a regular contributor to stickyminds.com and Better Software magazine and author of the upcoming business novel Rolling Rocks Downhill.

Clarke can be contacted at clarke.ching@spiceupIT.com.

www.RocksIntoGold.com